AF270414

LOS ANGELES

DODGERS

BY ANTHONY K. HEWSON

SportsZone

An Imprint of Abdo Publishing
abdobooks.com

abdobooks.com

Published by Abdo Publishing, a division of ABDO, PO Box 398166, Minneapolis, Minnesota 55439. Copyright © 2023 by Abdo Consulting Group, Inc. International copyrights reserved in all countries. No part of this book may be reproduced in any form without written permission from the publisher. SportsZone™ is a trademark and logo of Abdo Publishing.

Printed in China.
102022
012023

Cover Photo: Brandon Sloter/Icon Sportswire/Getty Images
Interior Photos: Kelly Gavin/MLB Photos/Getty Images, 4, 40; Cooper Neill/MLB Photos/Getty Images, 6; Mark Rucker/Transcendental Graphics/Getty Images Sport/Getty Images, 8, 11, 23; George Rinhart/Corbis Historical/Getty Images, 10; The Stanley Weston Archive/Archive Photos/Getty Images, 13; Bettmann/Getty Images, 14, 17, 18, 24; Bettmann Archive/Bettmann/Getty Images, 21; NY Daily News Archive/New York Daily News/Getty Images, 22; Hy Peskin/Archive Photos/Getty Images, 26; Focus On Sport/Getty Images, 28; Ron Vesely/MLB Photos/Getty Images Sport/Getty Images, 31, 34; Focus On Sport/Getty Images Sport/Getty Images, 32; Jayne Kamin-Oncea/Getty Images Sport/Getty Images, 33; Lucy Nicholson/AFP/Getty Images, 37; Kevork Djansezian/Getty Images Sport/Getty Images, 39

Editor: Steph Giedd
Series Designer: Becky Daum

Library of Congress Control Number: 2022940478

Publisher's Cataloging-in-Publication Data

Names: Hewson, Anthony K., author.
Title: Los Angeles Dodgers / by Anthony K. Hewson
Description: Minneapolis, Minnesota: Abdo Publishing, 2023 | Series: Inside MLB | Includes online resources and index.
Identifiers: ISBN 9781098290214 (lib. bdg.) | ISBN 9781098275419 (ebook)
Subjects: LCSH: Los Angeles Dodgers (Baseball team)--Juvenile literature. | Baseball teams--Juvenile literature. | Professional sports--Juvenile literature. | Sports franchises--Juvenile literature. | Major League Baseball (Organization)--Juvenile literature.
Classification: DDC 796.35764--dc23

CONTENTS

BORN IN BROOKLYN

The situation might have been funny if there wasn't so much on the line. The Los Angeles Dodgers trailed the Atlanta Braves 2–1 in the top of the sixth inning of Game 5 in the 2020 National League Championship Series (NLCS). At the plate for the Dodgers was catcher Will Smith. On the mound for Atlanta was a left-hander. Oddly, his name was also Will Smith.

Never had two players with the same name faced each other in a baseball playoff contest. And it just so happened to come at the biggest point in the game. Atlanta led the series 3–1. The Dodgers had two runners on with two outs. Los Angeles had been the heavy favorite to reach the World Series when the playoffs began. A championship would

Dodgers catcher Will Smith hit two homers and drove in 13 runs during the 2020 Major League Baseball (MLB) playoffs.

Smith celebrates with his teammates after his three-run homer in the sixth inning of Game 5 of the 2020 NLCS.

be the Dodgers' first since 1988. And they had lost two heartbreaking World Series in 2017 and 2018. Now the Dodgers needed to rally to keep their season alive. They needed their catcher William D. Smith to get a big hit off of Atlanta pitcher William M. Smith.

Atlanta's pitcher got two quick strikes on the Dodgers' catcher. Then two fastballs came up and in to the right-handed hitter, both backing the Los Angeles catcher off the plate. A 2–2 slider dropped low and inside, running the count full.

Due to the COVID-19 pandemic, the game was being played at Globe Life Field in Arlington, Texas. A crowd of just over

11,000 fans watched nervously as the battle played out. The Atlanta pitcher tried to come back with a knee-high fastball. The Dodgers' Smith dropped the barrel of his bat down and launched the ball to left-center field.

The shot cleared the fence for Smith's first career playoff home run. Suddenly the Dodgers led 4–2. It was still a long way back for a team with championship dreams. But one of playoff baseball's most unique moments was just the spark Los Angeles needed.

NAME GAME

Los Angeles has been the Dodgers' home for more than 60 years. However, the history of the team dates to the 1880s. And it began 3,000 miles (4,800 km) away from Southern California.

Baseball spread around New York City like wildfire in the 1800s. Clubs popped up everywhere, including dozens in the borough of Brooklyn, but only one team thrived and became a professional team.

THE RULES OF THE GAME

Baseball's true origins are unknown, but the borough of Brooklyn helped make the sport we know today. In 1857 the National Association of Base Ball Players (NABBP) met for the first time. The organization's 16 teams set rules for the 90-foot distance between bases, nine-inning games, and nine-man lineups, among other things. Of the 16 teams at the meeting, seven called Brooklyn home.

The 1903 Brooklyn Superbas team photos are shown in the *Sporting Life* newspaper.

Brooklyn's first major professional team began playing in 1884. The new club played in the American Association (AA).

At the time, team nicknames weren't formal as they are now. Some called the Brooklyn team the "Atlantics," others called the squad the "Grays." By the time the team joined the National League (NL) in 1890, many people called them the

"Bridegrooms" or simply "Grooms." The story goes that several of the team's players got married during the offseason before the 1888 season, and the new name stuck.

The Bridegrooms won the NL in their first season, even playing in an early version of the World Series. But that would be their best season until 1899, when the team finished 101–47 and won the NL easily. That year they had another new unofficial nickname. They went by "Superbas" after the name of a popular group of Broadway entertainers of the era.

At the time, the NL was the only major league. There was no World Series to play in. And by the time the American League (AL) was founded as a competitor to the NL, the Superbas were falling out of contention. In the year of the first modern World Series, in 1903, Brooklyn finished fifth in an eight-team NL.

EBBETS FIELD

It took a while for Brooklyn to get out of the basement. But even when it struggled, the team had a committed owner. Charles Ebbets had owned some stake in the team since the 1890s. By the early 1900s, he was majority owner and team president. One of his biggest dreams was to build the club a grand stadium. After slowly buying up land in Brooklyn, he finally had enough space to start construction. The result was Ebbets Field, one of the finest ballparks of its time.

Starting in 1913, Brooklyn spent 45 seasons playing at Ebbets Field.

Originally seating 23,000 people, it was then expanded to seat a little more than 31,000 fans. The stadium was huge for that era. Over the next half-century, it became one of the most beloved arenas in American sports.

Ebbets Field opened in 1913. Within four seasons, it saw a World Series game. The 1916 Brooklyn team had two excellent outfielders in Zack Wheat and Casey Stengel. It also featured a dominant pitching staff. Because the team was led by manager

Wilbert Robinson, fans called them the "Robins." After finishing 94–60, Brooklyn reached the World Series. There the Robins were beaten 4–1 by the Boston Red Sox.

Another trip to the World Series came four years later. The 1920 series was a best-of-nine matchup with the Cleveland Indians. Even though Robinson was still the manager, Brooklyn now had two widely used nicknames. Some called them the Robins, but others liked "Dodgers." That nickname had first popped up in the 1890s. It was a short version of "Trolley Dodgers." The nickname came from pedestrians in Brooklyn, who had to constantly move out of the way of passing trolley cars on the street. Whatever its nickname, Brooklyn came up short again. Cleveland won the series 5–2.

Outfielder Zack Wheat played 18 of his 19 MLB seasons with Brooklyn, and he led the NL with a .335 batting average in 1918.

DEM BUMS

Ebbets died in 1925. He never got to see his team play in the World Series again. In fact, throughout the 1920s, the Dodgers were known for bad baseball. Despite having superstars like outfielder Babe Herman and pitcher Dazzy Vance, Brooklyn finished higher than fifth only once for the rest of the decade. The team was known for making silly mistakes. On one famous play in 1926, the Dodgers ended up with three men standing on third base all at the same time.

Robinson's last year as manager was 1931. The next year, the Dodgers nickname became official. It started showing up on the team's uniforms in 1932. But the fans still came up with other terms for the fumbling team. Their many mistakes earned the nickname "the Daffiness Boys."

The most famous term of endearment for the team came from a sports cartoonist for the *New York World-Telegram* named Willard Mullin. He drew up a character called the "Brooklyn Bum." From then on, fans referred to the Dodgers as "Dem Bums."

Mullin's nickname was supposed to be an insult. And as the Dodgers lost their way through the 1930s, most fans used it that way. But the team was about to change everything, on and off the field, and turn the "Dem Bums" insult into a point of pride for Brooklyn.

Brooklyn pitcher Dazzy Vance was the 1924 NL MVP after leading the NL in wins, earned-run average (ERA), and strikeouts.

14

CHAPTER 2

CHANGING THE GAME

By the winter of 1942, the Dodgers were a powerhouse. They had won 100 games each of the previous two seasons and reached the 1941 World Series, which ended in a five-game loss to the New York Yankees. They were no longer bums. Now, "Dem Bums" were a team the close-knit Brooklyn community rallied around. The Dodgers were the pride of the borough.

They also had a new general manager (GM). Branch Rickey was considered one of the greatest minds in baseball. In his time with the St. Louis Cardinals, Rickey had revolutionized baseball by creating the farm system to develop players. Now he brought his next batch of big ideas to Brooklyn.

Jackie Robinson poses before a game in 1949.

Among other things, he established a spring training base for the Dodgers at Vero Beach, Florida. That made Brooklyn the first team with a permanent spring training home. Many other teams followed, seeking out warmer southern climates.

RICKEY AND ROBINSON

Rickey's biggest idea was yet to come, however. No AL or NL team had signed a Black player in more than 50 years. There was no formal rule against it. Instead, owners had gone by what they called a "gentlemen's agreement" to bar Black stars from MLB.

In the 1940s, the call to end that racist policy was getting louder. Many MLB players said they would welcome Black teammates. Sportswriters wrote column after column in support of the idea. Rickey also thought the gentlemen's agreement was unjust, and he wanted to do something about it.

The top Black players were limited to the Negro Leagues. For two years, Rickey scouted the Negro Leagues, looking for the player he thought could break down the barrier. He needed someone with not only talent but also the mental strength to handle the attention and abuse that was sure to come. In 1945 Rickey landed on Jack Roosevelt "Jackie" Robinson of the Kansas City Monarchs.

Dodgers President Branch Rickey, *right*, and team manager Burt Shotton, *left*, look on as Robinson, *center*, signs his contract for the 1949 season.

Robinson had played professional baseball for only one season. But he had been a superstar three-sport athlete at the University of California, Los Angeles (UCLA). He'd also shown his character by standing up to racist policies while in the army. Rickey called Robinson in for a meeting late in 1945. There the GM told him what to expect and how hard it would be. Robinson agreed to sign up for the plan.

After a year in the minors in 1946, Robinson was ready. He joined the Dodgers for the 1947 season. It wasn't an easy transition. Some of his own teammates started a petition saying they didn't want Robinson there. But Dodgers

Robinson, *right*, led the NL with 29 stolen bases during his 1947 Rookie of the Year season with Brooklyn.

management told players that Robinson was going to play. They had better get used to it.

HISTORIC DEBUT

On April 15, 1947, Robinson was in the lineup at Ebbets Field, playing first base. More than half of the 26,000 fans in the stands were Black. Robinson went 0-for-3 in a Dodgers win. Two days later he got his first MLB hit.

Throughout the season, Robinson endured racist abuse everywhere he went. Through it all, he kept his agreement with Rickey not to fight back at any point. The GM and player both knew that if Robinson retaliated, he would take the blame. The plan would fail.

Under extreme pressure, Robinson played incredible baseball. He hit .297 and stole a league-high 29 bases. At the end of the season, he had played a huge role in getting the Dodgers back to the World Series. That year the Rookie of the Year Award was given out in MLB for the first time. It went to Robinson. But most important, he had changed baseball forever.

WAIT 'TIL NEXT YEAR

The Dodgers lost the 1947 World Series in seven games to the Yankees. That set up a familiar theme. For the next decade, Brooklyn was good enough every year to compete. It had a lineup featuring Robinson, shortstop Pee Wee Reese, and first baseman Gil Hodges. Carl Furillo and Duke Snider were superstar outfielders. Preacher Roe and Ralph Branca were standout pitchers. And Robinson was soon joined by other Black stars like ace pitcher Don Newcombe and catcher Roy Campanella.

However, the Dodgers could not find a way to win it all. They lost to the Yankees again in 1949. In 1951 they were

GOLDEN VOICES

In 1939 the Dodgers hired radio broadcaster Red Barber. The Mississippi-born play-by-play man was known for his laid-back personality and several unique phrases. He left the team in 1953, giving way to Vin Scully, who had been working for the Dodgers with Barber since 1950. The native New Yorker Scully went on to call Dodgers games until 2016. In addition, Scully became one of the most recognizable voices in sports while calling several World Series on radio and television. Today he is considered the best play-by-play voice in baseball history.

13 games ahead of their NL rivals, the New York Giants, in mid-August. But Brooklyn collapsed and lost the lead. The Giants then won a three-game playoff on a dramatic walk-off home run by third baseman Bobby Thomson. The homer is still known as "the Shot Heard 'round the World."

The Dodgers shook off that disappointment to reach the World Series in 1952. They had a 3–2 lead on the Yankees before losing in seven games. In 1953 the Yankees beat Brooklyn 4–2.

Dodgers and Yankees fans lived right next to each other in New York City. When Yankees fans would taunt Dodgers rooters, Brooklyn fans could only fire back, "Wait 'til next year!" It became a common slogan for the Dodgers.

NEXT YEAR

In 1955 the Dodgers met the Yankees in the World Series yet again. Despite Robinson thrilling fans by stealing home in Game 1, the Dodgers lost. It looked like another disappointment when New York took Game 2 as well. But lefty Johnny Podres got the Dodgers back in it with an 8–3 complete game victory in Game 3. The Dodgers went on to win the next two games, also at Ebbets Field.

The Yankees took Game 6 to force a decisive seventh game. Podres had been inconsistent during the regular season,

finishing just 9–10. But
manager Walter Alston
played a hunch and
went with Podres over
Newcombe, who had been
roughed up in the series.

Alston's idea worked.
Podres pitched a
masterpiece. He kept the
Yankees off balance all
game. The main trouble
he ran into was in the
bottom of the sixth. The
Yankees put two men on
with no one out. New York

Johnny Podres allowed eight hits and struck out four Yankees during his complete game win in Game 7 of the 1955 World Series.

catcher Yogi Berra drilled a deep fly ball to the left-field corner.
Substitute left fielder Sandy Amoros tracked it down and made
a difficult catch, then hurled the ball back to the infield. Reese
relayed it to Hodges at first for a double play. Podres retired
the next man to get out of the inning.

The Dodgers scratched out two runs of their own. And
Podres pitched his second complete game of the series. At long
last, Brooklyn was a winner. The *New York Daily News* headline
the next day read, "This Is Next Year."

Dodgers players rush to Podres after he got the final out to win the 1955 World Series.

Podres had saved the Dodgers with two amazing pitching performances. For his efforts, he earned a new award given out that year. Podres was the first Most Valuable Player (MVP) in World Series history.

ROBINSON'S LEGACY

The Dodgers reached the World Series again in 1956. It was their seventh appearance in 16 years. This time they again lost to the Yankees. The series proved to be the last MLB appearance for Jackie Robinson. At 37 years old, he was slowing down as a player. After the season, he decided to retire.

His impact on the game was incredible. Just months after he played his first game, Cleveland called up Larry Doby. Doby, a versatile infielder turned outfielder in 1948, became the first Black player in the AL.

By the time Robinson left baseball, nearly every team had Black players. And many of them, like the Giants' Willie Mays and Ernie Banks of the Chicago Cubs, were superstars.

Jackie Robinson was inducted into the National Baseball Hall of Fame in 1962.

Robinson left baseball with successes that included a batting championship and an MVP Award. But more important, he had made it possible for others to follow him. In 2004 MLB declared April 15, the anniversary of his first game, as "Jackie Robinson Day." All players on every team wear his uniform number, 42, for their games. That number has been retired throughout baseball. Aside from April 15, no player will ever wear No. 42 again as a tribute to baseball's pioneer.

CHAPTER 3

LA LA LAND

In the 1950s, New York ruled the baseball world. The New York Yankees, New York Giants, and Brooklyn Dodgers were all powerhouse teams. But the two NL teams had a common problem. Both of their stadiums were getting old.

Ebbets Field had begun construction in 1912. The Giants' home of the Polo Grounds had existed in some form since the 1890s. For the Dodgers, the size of Ebbets Field was another problem. When it was built, the park was one of the largest in baseball. Now it was considered small.

All of this resulted in Dodgers owner Walter O'Malley losing money. Making matters worse was that both he and Giants owner Horace Stoneham saw big profits available across

Hall of Fame slugger Duke Snider led the NL with 43 home runs in 1956.

Left fielder Wally Moon, *at bat*, played seven of his 12 MLB seasons with the Dodgers. He led the majors in triples (11) in 1959.

the country. California's population was growing every year. And baseball would soon find its way there.

The unthinkable happened to Brooklyn in 1957. O'Malley decided to move the Dodgers to Los Angeles. The Giants were also moving to San Francisco. The loss of both teams sent shock waves through New York.

The moves were instantly popular in California, however. The Dodgers hosted the Giants on April 18, 1958. Los Angeles's home opener drew 78,672 fans to watch a 6–5 Dodgers win.

Los Angeles didn't have to wait long for a winner. In 1959 the Dodgers reached the World Series against the Chicago

White Sox. Chicago blew out Los Angeles 11–0 in Game 1. But Johnny Podres and reliever Larry Sherry held down the White Sox in Game 2 as the Dodgers rallied from an early 2–0 hole to win 4–3. Los Angeles won the next two games, and a World Series–record crowd of 92,706 fans showed up for Game 5. They hoped to witness the first championship on the West Coast, but the Dodgers lost 1–0. Los Angeles finished off the victory in Chicago in Game 6. Home runs by center fielder Duke Snider, left fielder Wally Moon, and pinch-hitter Chuck Essegian highlighted a 9–3 blowout.

PITCHING RICH

Snider was 32 that season, while Gil Hodges was 35. Soon it would be time for a new set of stars to take over. And Los Angeles had two great pitchers already on its roster.

Righty Don Drysdale went 17–13 in 1959. The 22-year-old also led the league in strikeouts while making his first All-Star team. Drysdale threw hard, and he was not shy about hitting batters. By the time he retired, he had drilled a modern NL record of 154 hitters. It was all part of his pitching strategy. Drysdale didn't want hitters comfortable in the batter's box.

By 1961 Drysdale had a perfect running mate on the mound in lefty Sandy Koufax. The shy, skinny pitcher had debuted as a 19-year-old in 1955. Through the 1959 season, Koufax had

Dodger pitchers Don Drysdale, *left*, and Sandy Koufax, *right*, dominated the NL in the early 1960s.

a record of only 28–27. His main problem was that he was too wild. Koufax walked nearly as many batters as he struck out. Frustrated, he was thinking about quitting baseball.

In 1961 a catcher told Koufax that he should try not throwing as hard. Koufax had a lightning arm, and he could still dominate without overdoing it. The plan worked. Koufax soon put together six of the best pitching seasons ever. He led the NL in ERA every year from 1962 to 1966. After Drysdale won 25 games and the Cy Young Award in 1962, Koufax truly took over. He won the award in 1963, 1965, and 1966. Each year he won at least 25 games. In 1965 Koufax struck out a record 382 batters.

Those pitching performances helped the Dodgers sweep the 1963 World Series over the Yankees. In 1965 Koufax pitched a three-hit shutout on two days' rest in Game 7 as the Dodgers beat the Minnesota Twins for another World Series title.

After the 1966 season, Koufax abruptly retired. He had been pitching with arm pain for years and had finally had enough. He was just 30 years old when he walked away from the game.

WALTER WALKS AWAY

The Dodgers remained near the top of the NL through the rest of the 1960s and 1970s. They went back to the World Series in 1974 but lost to another new California team, the Oakland Athletics. That proved to be the last World Series for longtime manager Walter Alston. The 62-year-old had been in the Dodgers' dugout since 1954. He had led the team to championships in both Brooklyn and Los Angeles. When he decided to leave during the final week of the 1976 season, Alston had won 2,040 games. His replacement was Tommy Lasorda, who had been with the Dodgers off and on as a player, scout, and coach since 1949. The new manager soon had the Dodgers back on top.

FERNANDOMANIA

Lasorda led the Dodgers to the World Series in both 1977 and 1978. Both years they were beaten by the Yankees. The old New York rivalry now stretched across the country.

In 1981 the teams met again. The year had been a strange one. A players' strike halfway through the year shortened the Dodgers' season to 110 games. But that was more than enough time for Los Angeles to fall in love with a new pitching star.

Rookie Fernando Valenzuela took the majors by storm in 1981. The left-hander finished 13–7 with a 2.48 ERA and eight shutouts in 25 starts. Beyond his numbers, he won over fans with his unique windup. As he turned his body to load up for a pitch, Valenzuela looked up to the sky instead of at home plate.

His fame became known as "Fernandomania." Dodgers fans adored their new star. This was particularly true in Los Angeles's Latino community. Valenzuela, who had been born in Mexico, was a cultural hero.

The Dodgers had to sweat out two five-game playoff rounds against the Houston Astros and Montreal Expos to get back to the World Series. Valenzuela won key games both times. In the NLCS, outfielder Rick Monday backed Valenzuela up with a tiebreaking home run in the ninth inning of Game 5 in Montreal.

Valenzuela also won Game 3 of the World Series against the Yankees after New York had opened up a 2–0 lead. The Dodgers followed up Valenzuela's win by sweeping the rest of the series for their first title since 1965.

UNBELIEVABLE

It took Los Angeles seven more years to reach the

Fernando Valenzuela led the NL with 11 complete games in 1981.

World Series again. In 1988 the Dodgers did not have a great team. But they had two great players. Hard-nosed outfielder Kirk Gibson led the Dodgers with 25 home runs and was the team's emotional leader. Pitcher Orel Hershiser won the Cy Young Award by finishing 23–8 with 15 complete games. During the season, Hershiser set an MLB record by pitching

59 straight innings without allowing a run. The old record of 58 2/3 had been held by Drysdale.

The Dodgers upset the New York Mets in the NLCS to reach the World Series against the Athletics. Oakland was another heavy favorite. This was even more true after Gibson suffered injuries to both legs in the NLCS. As the World Series opened, the star outfielder was not likely to play.

However, Gibson surprised everyone by pinch hitting in the bottom of the ninth inning in Game 1. The Dodgers were down 4–3 with two outs and a runner on first. Gibson would have to face Dennis Eckersley, Oakland's excellent closer.

Visibly hobbling, Gibson battled Eckersley by fouling off several pitches. On the eighth pitch, the left-handed Gibson muscled a ball to right field. Astonished fans at Dodger

Stadium watched the ball sail over the fence. One of the most dramatic home runs in World Series history had won the game 5–4.

Legendary announcer, Jack Buck, calling the game on the radio, screamed, "I don't believe what I just saw!" On the national television broadcast of the game, Vin Scully wondered whether Gibson would be able to make it back to home plate after watching the Dodgers' star limp around the bases.

Pitcher Orel Hershiser, *left*, celebrates with Dodgers catcher Rick Dempsey, *center*, and first baseman Franklin Stubbs, *right*, after the final out of the 1988 World Series.

Gibson did not play again in the series. But it didn't matter. Hershiser took over and won Game 2 with a 6–0 shutout. He pitched again in Game 5 with Los Angeles up 3–1. The righty closed out the upset by striking out nine batters in another complete game.

CHAPTER 4

DODGER BLUE

Manager Tommy Lasorda was so loyal to the Dodgers that he famously said he "bled Dodger Blue." And throughout his two decades in charge, the team was almost always successful. However, in the early 1990s he led Los Angeles through a down stretch. In 1992 the Dodgers suffered 99 losses, their most since they were called the Brooklyn Superbas in 1908.

It didn't take long for Los Angeles to recover. By 1995 Lasorda had the team back in the playoffs. But the next year he suffered a heart attack and had to step away from managing. After the year was over, Lasorda decided it was time to give the manager's job to someone else. Bill Russell, who filled in while

Dodgers catcher Mike Piazza was the 1993 NL Rookie of the Year.

Lasorda was out, was given the job. Russell was just the third manager the Dodgers had hired in 43 years.

BIG MONEY

A new manager wasn't the only change for the team in the late 1990s. The O'Malley family had controlled the Dodgers since 1950. In 1998 they decided to sell. Billionaire Rupert Murdoch bought the team. The Dodgers had a rich owner in addition to playing in a huge city. That meant they had money to spend.

Los Angeles took on high-priced stars like sluggers Gary Sheffield and Bobby Bonilla. Then they made pitcher Kevin Brown the first $100-million player in MLB history. But the payouts didn't work. Los Angeles missed the playoffs for seven straight years starting in 1997.

Some of the Dodgers' best players were still the ones who came through the team's farm system. Catcher Paul Lo Duca, third baseman Adrián Beltré, and closer Éric Gagné were all key players when the team won the NL West Division in 2004.

LATE ROUND GEM

One of the Dodgers' best pickups in the 1990s was catcher Mike Piazza, who was selected in the 62nd round of the 1988 draft. Piazza made his debut in 1992 and hit 177 home runs in seven years with the team. Later it came out that the Dodgers only drafted Piazza as a favor to his father, who was a close friend of Tommy Lasorda.

Éric Gagné led MLB with 55 saves in 2003 on his way to winning that year's NL Cy Young Award.

All three were either drafted by Los Angeles or signed as amateur free agents.

The Dodgers kept trying to break through during the 2000s, making the playoffs three more times. But each time, they came up short of the World Series. Big-name players like pitcher Greg Maddux, outfielder Manny Ramirez, and center fielder Andruw Jones all showed up in Los Angeles. But none of them could put the Dodgers over the top.

SOUTHPAW SUPERSTAR

The 2008 Dodgers reached the NLCS with the help of a 20-year-old left-handed pitcher. Clayton Kershaw had been the team's first-round draft pick in 2006, but he didn't join the team until late May of 2008. Down the stretch that season, Kershaw went 5–5 and showed promise by striking out 100 batters in 107 1/3 innings.

Within four years, Kershaw was the best pitcher in the NL. He finished 21–5 with a 2.28 ERA and 248 strikeouts to win his first Cy Young Award in 2011. Kershaw was the next great ace in the team's long line of them.

The Dodgers made it back to the playoffs in 2013, losing the NLCS to the St. Louis Cardinals. That started a frustrating pattern in Los Angeles. The Dodgers won the NL West every year. But they fell flat in the playoffs. In 2014 and 2015, they were upset in the NL Division Series (NLDS). The 2016 season saw the Dodgers fall short in the NLCS. The old Brooklyn saying of "Wait 'til next year" showed up again. Like the team, Kershaw often struggled in the postseason, giving up big innings in several starts.

WORLD SERIES CONTROVERSIES

Finally, in 2017, the Dodgers reached the World Series again. Their opponents were the Houston Astros. The teams slugged their way through seven games. But Houston came out on top 5–1 in Game 7 at Dodger Stadium.

Two years after the series, a story broke that the Astros had been using technology to steal opponents' signs in 2017. The scandal started a debate that Houston should be stripped of its title, awarding the trophy to the Dodgers.

The Dodgers also lost the 2018 World Series to the Boston Red Sox, who were found to have stolen signs during the regular season as well. Once again there were calls that the Dodgers were the rightful champions. But MLB commissioner Rob Manfred refused to strip either Houston or Boston of their wins. Boston was given a lesser punishment since they stopped breaking the rule after the regular season.

Clayton Kershaw won his third NL Cy Young Award in 2014.

Mookie Betts celebrates after hitting a homer in Game 1 of the 2020 World Series.

AT LONG LAST

The start of the 2020 season was delayed from April to July due to the COVID-19 pandemic. But the Dodgers showed up ready to go, starting the season 30–10 and finishing 43–17. The offense was aided by former AL MVP outfielder Mookie Betts, who joined from the Red Sox in a blockbuster trade. He was one of five Dodgers who hit at least 12 home runs for manager Dave Roberts. Kershaw still anchored the starting staff. But he was joined by young stars like righty Walker Buehler and lefty Julio Urías.

The Dodgers did not lose a game in either the NL wild-card series or the NLDS. Catcher Will Smith's home run in Game 5 sparked a comeback in the NLCS. The Dodgers were back in the World Series.

Kershaw got them off to a good start with eight strikeouts over six innings in Game 1 to defeat the Tampa Bay Rays 8–3. Heading into Game 4, the Dodgers were up 2–1. In the bottom of the ninth inning, the Dodgers threw away a 7–6 lead on a wild play. Tampa Bay's Brett Phillips singled with runners on first and second. The first runner scored, and then two Dodgers errors allowed the next runner to score.

Despite the crushing loss, Kershaw got Los Angeles back on track in Game 5. Backed by an early 3–0 lead, he took the game into the sixth. The Dodgers won 4–2 to move one step from a title.

The Rays took an early 1–0 lead in Game 6. But a wild pitch in the bottom of the sixth helped Los Angeles take a 2–1 lead. Betts put it away in the eighth with a long home run to left-center field. He let out a huge scream coming around first base as the ball went over the fence. On the mound, Urías shut down the Rays over the final 2 1/3 innings. His fourth strikeout ended the game and 31 years of frustration in Los Angeles.

The Dodgers continued their successful ways after the World Series victory. In 2021 they tied a franchise mark with 106 wins. In 2022 Los Angeles broke that record with 111 victories. But the Dodgers failed to reach the World Series in both seasons. Still, for one of baseball's most storied clubs, there was always next year.

TIMELINE

1884

The franchise is founded as the Brooklyn Atlantics.

1913

Ebbets Field opens in Brooklyn.

1916

As the Brooklyn Robins, the team reaches its first World Series but loses to the Boston Red Sox.

1932

After the departure of manager Wilbert Robinson, the Robins are renamed the Dodgers.

1942

Owner Walter O'Malley hires Branch Rickey as general manager.

1947

Jackie Robinson becomes the first Black player in the AL or NL in the 20th century and wins Rookie of the Year honors while leading the Dodgers to the World Series.

1955

The Dodgers finally break through and win their first World Series.

1959

One year after relocating to Los Angeles, the Dodgers win their second World Series title.

1965

Led by pitchers Sandy Koufax and Don Drysdale, Los Angeles wins its third championship in seven years.

1976

Walter Alston retires after 23 years as team manager and is replaced by third base coach Tommy Lasorda.

1981

In the grip of "Fernandomania," Los Angeles defeats the New York Yankees to win the World Series.

1988

Kirk Gibson's dramatic Game 1 home run highlights the Dodgers' five-game upset of the Oakland Athletics in the World Series.

1996

Health problems force Lasorda to step down as Dodgers' manager after 21 years in charge.

1998

The O'Malley family sells the Dodgers after 48 years of ownership.

2013

Led by ace pitcher Clayton Kershaw, Los Angeles wins the first of eight straight NL West titles.

2020

After years of playoff frustration, the Dodgers defeat the Tampa Bay Rays 4–2 in the World Series.

2022

Los Angeles wins a franchise-record 111 games during the regular season, but the team falls short of reaching the World Series.

TEAM FACTS

FRANCHISE HISTORY

Brooklyn Atlantics (1884)
Brooklyn Grays (1885–87)
Brooklyn Bridegrooms
    (1888–90, 1896–98)
Brooklyn Grooms (1891–95)
Brooklyn Superbas
    (1899–1910, 1913)
Brooklyn Dodgers (1911–12,
    1932–57)
Brooklyn Robins (1914–31)
Los Angeles Dodgers (1958–)

WORLD SERIES CHAMPIONSHIPS

1955, 1959, 1963, 1965, 1981,
1988, 2020

KEY PLAYERS

Mookie Betts (2020–)
Roy Campanella (1948–57)
Don Drysdale (1956–69)
Carl Furillo (1946–60)
Orel Hershiser (1983–94, 2000)
Gil Hodges (1943, 1947–61)
Clayton Kershaw (2008–)

Sandy Koufax (1955–66)
Don Newcombe (1949–51,
    1954–58)
Pee Wee Reese (1940–42,
    1946–58)
Jackie Robinson (1947–56)
Duke Snider (1947–62)
Don Sutton (1966–80, 1988)
Fernando Valenzuela
    (1980–90)

KEY MANAGERS

Walter Alston (1954–76)
Tommy Lasorda (1976–96)
Dave Roberts (2016–)
Wilbert Robinson (1914–31)

HOME STADIUMS

Washington Park I (1884–90)
Ridgewood Park (1886–89)
Eastern Park (1891–97)
Washington Park II (1898–1912)
Ebbets Field (1913–1957)
Roosevelt Stadium (1956–57)
Los Angeles Memorial
    Coliseum (1958–61)
Dodger Stadium (1962–)

RUBBER ARM

Dodgers pitcher Mike Marshall didn't have much time off during the 1974 season. Marshall appeared in 106 games out of the bullpen, a record for an MLB pitcher. He stayed effective, finishing 15–12 with a 2.42 ERA. Marshall was the first reliever ever to win the Cy Young Award.

YOUNG LEGEND

Players are eligible for the Hall of Fame after they have been retired for five years. Because of his early retirement, Sandy Koufax became eligible when he was just 36 years old. He was elected on his first try, in 1972. That made Koufax the youngest player ever enshrined in Cooperstown, New York.

WALTER'S WAY

Walter Alston managed the Dodgers from 1954 to 1976. His 23 seasons in charge of one team are the third most in MLB history. Only Connie Mack (50 years with the Philadelphia Athletics) and John McGraw (31 years with the New York Giants) managed a single team longer.

ROOKIES OF THE YEAR

From 1992 through 1996, every NL Rookie of the Year played for the Dodgers. First baseman Eric Karros started the record streak. He was followed by catcher Mike Piazza, outfielder Raúl Mondesí, pitcher Hideo Nomo, and outfielder Todd Hollandsworth.

GLOSSARY

ace

A team's best starting pitcher.

amateur

A person who plays a sport without getting paid.

borough

A section of New York City that also makes up its own county.

closer

A pitcher who comes in at the end of the game to secure a win for his team.

commissioner

The chief executive of a sports league.

farm system

In baseball, all the minor league teams that feed players to one major league team.

free agents

Players whose rights are not owned by any team.

pandemic

A widespread outbreak of a disease that affects a large portion of the population.

players' strike

When players refuse to work due to a disagreement between them and their employers (teams) about things such as working conditions or wages.

rookie

A professional athlete in his or her first year of competition.

shutout

A complete game in which a team allows no runs.

walk-off

Any victory in which the home team scores the winning run in the bottom of the final inning.

MORE INFORMATION

BOOKS

Flynn, Brendan. *The MLB Encyclopedia*. Minneapolis, MN: Abdo Publishing, 2022.

Harris, Duchess, JD, PhD with Alex Kies. *The Negro Leagues*. Minneapolis, MN: Abdo Publishing, 2020.

Hewson, Anthony K. *GOATs of Baseball*. Minneapolis, MN: Abdo Publishing, 2022.

ONLINE RESOURCES

To learn more about the Los Angeles Dodgers, please visit **abdobooklinks.com** or scan this QR code. These links are routinely monitored and updated to provide the most current information available.

ABOUT THE AUTHOR

Anthony K. Hewson is a freelance writer who specializes in writing nonfiction for kids.